Accomplish What You Will

ONE WOMAN'S LIFE'S JOURNEY AND LEGACY

By
B GILWARDS

Conscious Dreams
PUBLISHING

Accomplish What You Will
One Woman's Life's Journey and Legacy

Copyright © 2024: B Gilwards

All rights reserved. No part of this publication may be produced, distributed, or transmitted in any form or by any means, including photocopying, recording, or other electronic or mechanical methods, without the prior written permission of the publisher, except in the case of brief quotations embodied in critical reviews and certain other non-commercial uses permitted by copyright law.

Any resemblance to names, characters, and incidents portrayed in this book is totally coincidental.

First Printed in United Kingdom 2024

Published by Conscious Dreams Publishing
www.consciousdreamspublishing.com

Edited by Elise Abram and Daniella Blechner
Cover Design by Emily Rakic
Book Interior and E-book Design by Amit Dey

ISBN: 978-1-915522-55-9

ACKNOWLEDGEMENTS

I give thanks to my Creator and Ancestors.
I also thank my family and friends,
including Nkechi Aligbe-Abeng

*'Champions aren't made in the gyms.
Champions are made from something they have deep inside them,
a desire, a dream, a vision.'*

Muhammad Ali (boxer)

*'We truly are natural, pure, beautiful, and powerful.
The trouble is some of us are not aware of it.'*

B Gilwards

TABLE OF CONTENTS

PART ONE

The Becoming of Patience 1

1. The Early Days 7

2. The Taste of Independence 19

3. The Awakening 25

4 The Meeting 29

5. The Return Home 35

PART TWO

Soul to Soul 39

6. The Wedding 45

7. Post Honeymoon 51

8. The Passing 55

9. Time Out 57

PART THREE

Hope in the Midst of Despair 59

10. The Journey 63

PART FOUR

The Legacy 67

11. Epilogue 71

Part One

THE BECOMING OF PATIENCE

The blue sky was unblemished. The birds, grasshoppers, mosquitoes, goats, and others chatted in their respective languages whilst the eclectic flowers exhaled their fragrances.

I had retained my tall, slim frame. My hair was natural, short and peppered with silver. Our four grandchildren—six-year-old identical twin grandsons, Kwame and Kehinde, and ten and twelve-year-old granddaughters, Abena and Afryea—sat at my feet on the veranda, which was kept cool with the aid of ceiling fans.

I shared with them my family autobiography, gently turning the pages of the bulky but tidy photo album.

'Well.' I began after adjusting the cushion in a comfortable position behind me.

'As you know, African people travelled the world, with some living in Britain centuries and centuries ago.'

'That's a very long time ago,' said Abena. Abena was stout and wore mainly dresses. Her cane rows were tied up neatly with a red silk ribbon.

'A very, long, time ago,' said Kwame and Kehinde together with a giggle. The twins were medium-built, tall for their age, and took delight in dressing the same. They sometimes enjoyed teasing people who could not distinguish one from the other.

'My parents—your great-grandparents—travelled from Jamaica to England in the 1950s - known as the Windrush Generation. The British government at the time had invited people from the Caribbean and some other countries to help rebuild Britain after the Second World War. Your great-grandfather was a teacher and hoped to continue when he arrived, but like many from the Caribbean, the work available to them was in the public services: the hospitals, on trains or buses, in factories or as postal workers. Your great-grandmother was already a trained nurse, but she had to retrain, as did other nurses from the Caribbean. Although the training was the same, because back then, Britain owned much of the Caribbean. They had no choice; it was the only way they could continue to be nurses.'

'Why didn't great-grandfather retrain so he could carry on teaching?' Afryea enquired.

Afryea was short for her twelve years and had the strong, quiet demeanour of an eldest child. Like her sister, she had neat cane rows, except she wore a yellow ribbon.

'In those days,' I continued, 'for "Coloured people," as we were called then, our qualifications were not considered relevant or important. Many were employed in jobs they were overqualified for, like your great-grandfather working for the British Transport—the railway—which he did until he retired.'

I sipped some of my cool homemade carrot juice, then mopped the perspiration from my brow.

'Your great-grandparents lived with your great-grandfather's uncle, my great uncle, your great-great-great uncle Louie. He shared the house he owned with others who came from abroad to work and found it difficult to find accommodation because there were signs in windows that read, 'No Blacks. No Irish. No dogs.' Many assumed the house belonged to one of his Irish lodgers, but he was one of the few men of African heritage at the time who had managed to buy his own house.'

'Granny, why was it difficult for some people to find a place to live?' asked Abena.

'Perhaps it was because people were afraid and thought some Caribbean, African and some Irish people would still be angry for what had happened to their people and countries years before. Or perhaps they just feared the unknown—who knows?'

'We learnt in school that many African people were enslaved and treated very badly, and their countries were destroyed, causing disease and starvation,' informed Afryea whilst fanning away irritating mosquitoes.

'Yes. See? This is my great-uncle Louie. He was a pilot. He came from Jamaica on a ship called Empress of Australia in the 1940s, when people were invited from the "Commonwealth" countries to fight in the Second World War.'

'We learnt about that as well,' said Abena.

'Wow! Granny, why is the photo brown and beige?' asked Kwame.

'And this one of great-granny and granddad?' added Kehinde.

'That's because there weren't any colour photos back then, and although it's brown and beige, it was considered black and white,' I explained.

'Black and white?' asked the twins in unison, observing the photo of their great-great-great uncle Louie, standing next to a plane, looking handsome and proud in his Royal Air Force uniform.

'Our great-grandparents look like classic film stars, great-grandfather in his smart suit and great-grandmother in her lovely suit, high-heeled shoes, and handbag. Just like in those 1940s and 50s classic films,' Abena said with admiration.

'Your great-grandparents were a handsome couple, very close and loving. They moved out of great-great-great Uncle Louie's to live in a house they'd bought by saving each week with family and friends and taking it in turns to receive the full amount saved. This way of raising money is called "Pardner". It was difficult for people from the Caribbean to get money from banks in those days.

'This is the house.' I presented the black and white photo of the semi. 'There were three bedrooms and a living room we called the "best room." It was only used when we had visitors. As children, we weren't allowed in there without an adult. We also had a bathroom inside the house ----'

'Of course, it was *inside* the house,' interrupted Afryea, whilst giggling and unconsciously swatting a fly before it landed on her face.

'In those days, many people didn't have bathrooms and had to use the toilet, which was out in the garden.'

'In the garden? Wasn't it cold?' Kehinde was intrigued. The other children laughed.

I told them, 'Yes, sometimes it was, and at night, people used potties or buckets and then emptied them out in the mornings.'

'What about doing "big jobs? asked Kwame. He and the other children giggled.

'Only little children were allowed to do "big jobs" in potties. The grown-ups had to use the outside toilet, even when it was very cold and even in the middle of the night.' I proceeded to share an experience. 'I never used to go outside as I was always a little nervous in the dark, except for one night when, for some reason, I was feeling brave, so I stepped out into the darkness in the direction of the toilet. My heart was pounding so fast that I could feel it in my chest, but I kept going. I was nearly there when suddenly, a black cat jumped from a roof in front of me, startling me. All I could see were his green eyes. I screamed so loud that I woke my father, who came out and took me back into the house.'

The children giggled again.

'What's that?' Abena pointed to the photo of the living room, where crocheted, starched doilies had been placed on some of the mahogany furniture.

There were several china ornaments, displayed on a cabinet, itself filled with sets of china and glassware, only used on special occasions.

'Oh, the piano,' Afryea realised.

'Yes, your great-grandmother used to play, and her sister, great-great Aunty "Nessy", played. She also played the church organ.'

'Wow! There's the clock on the mantelpiece—is it the same one?' Abena enquired.

'Yes, but it doesn't work anymore,' I shared sadly as I recalled my father winding it with a key every Sunday morning just before taking himself and us off to church.

It was clear the grandchildren wanted to know more, so after giving them all a piece of fruit, some of my best ginger cake and a drink, I proceeded to share my story with them.

1

THE EARLY DAYS

'Focus on what matters and on the people who matter, despite the obstacles.'

~My parents

I was born in Maidstone, Kent, in England, in 1954 to Delbert and Winifred Walker, I have three younger siblings, each born a year apart. There's my brother, Winston, my sister, Faith and my youngest brother, Wilfred. Each of them inherited the Silver Cross pram that I was the first to 'christen'.

My father was tall, proud and quietly confident, a qualified teacher but was employed by British Rail. After a while, he grew used to the job and the teasing from his colleagues for his 'educated way of speaking.' Whilst this job was not ideal, it was stable, and had brought in a small but regular income. Due to the long hours, it was not possible for my father to attend night school and anyway there was no guarantee he would get a teaching post at the end of it.

My mother was medium built, assertive and very organised. She was a 'housewife' until she returned to nursing four nights per week when I was eight.

My parents could best be described as a 'refined couple' who did not show their affection by hugging and kissing their children or each other, but we all knew we were loved, and that our parents loved each other.

Winston, the eldest of my two brothers, was a miniature version of my father. He was also tall and slim, and followed him around, consciously and unconsciously imitating him.

Faith, my sister, was medium in build and very feminine. She enjoyed 'pretty things', including lacy dresses and dolls.

Wilfred, the baby of the family, was everyone's favourite and a little spoilt.

Many would say that I was a miniature version of my mother, enjoying the responsibility of looking after my siblings and undertaking household tasks. I also enjoyed reading. This sometimes caused annoyance for my family when I was so engrossed in whatever story I was reading and oblivious to the world around me.

Our family was a close one, and it functioned well with its routines, which included us being woken at a specific time when our father would give us breakfast. It was usually served around the same time our mother returned home from working at the local hospital. When our father left for work, our mother checked that Faith's and my plaited hair remained tidy with the aid of the knotted stocking tops we'd worn since the previous evening. She then escorted us to school.

Owning a twin tub made it easier for our mother to complete the laundry before going to bed. After some hours, she got up in time to prepare the evening meal and collect us from school. After our father returned home, everyone said grace— 'For health and strength and daily food, we praise thy name, oh Lord. Amen'—before each meal, and 'Thank and Praise the Lord' afterwards.

On Saturdays, Faith and I assisted our mother with the shopping and household tasks, whilst the boys assisted our father in washing and polishing the Morris Oxford Series Five and mowing the front and back lawns.

We did not receive pocket money for undertaking these tasks. We were, however, allowed to keep the money we earned from returning empty soft drink bottles to the corner shop. Sometimes, we saved the money in a miniature red metal letterbox. Other times, it was spent on fruit salad, pineapple chunks, sherbet fountains, and other sweets, none of which our parents approved. They encouraged healthier options of fruit and nuts, well before the 'Five a Day' had been introduced.

Late Saturday evenings, our family listened and danced to 'Doo Wop' and Blue Beat, and some years later, to Motown vinyl records, played on the sideboard-sized audiogram.

Our parents, other family members, and invited friends danced into the night. My siblings, I, and the children of those invited, watched from in between the stair bannisters when we should have long been asleep.

Every Sunday morning, we attended the local church led by the charismatic Pastor McHugh.

Faith and I wore lacy dresses with starched cotton under slips made by our mother, along with white socks, white shoes and matching handbags. Winston and Wilfred looked sharp in their little black suits, bow ties, and polished black shoes.

'T'ank you Jeezos,' 'Hallelujah,' and 'Praise de Lard,' were heard amongst members of the congregation as Pastor McHugh spoke eloquently with reference to the Bible and his knowledge from previous learning back in Jamaica. Traditional hymns and choruses were sung in harmony.

After church was dinner, play and relaxation in the form of visiting or entertaining other family members and friends.

Sometimes, there were outings to parks, zoos, various seasides and other places of interest in the gleaming black Morris Oxford.

These outings were sometimes by coach with the church, with Pastor McHugh, his wife—affectionately known as Miss Birdie, due to her fine-boned features—and their adopted son, Richard.

There was an occasion when Pastor McHugh and Miss Birdie organised a trip to the seaside. My siblings and I were so excited about going that we got up very early, although I had helped my mother prepare the fried chicken and fish fritters, sliced the hard-dough bread, bun, and cheese, and wrapped them in tinfoil the previous night. These were all placed in a basket with bottles of homemade carrot juice, which were kept cool in the kitchen pantry. We also packed everyone's swimming costumes and trunks, a bucket, a spade and a football into a large waterproof bag.

The arrangement was that those who were going to the seaside met in the church hall to wait for the coach to arrive at eight o' clock, with a view to leaving at eight thirty. Like most people, my family arrived on time. A couple were late, making the coach driver stop just as he was about to pull away.

On the coach, some people sang songs, which were led by Pastor McHugh, and some others chatted and laughed.

Upon arrival at the seaside, some of the women went to local shops to buy souvenirs, whilst some of the men were on the beach playing dominoes. The children made sandcastles, and some played football and cricket before the picnic lunch.

It was a fun day, enjoyed by all.

On the occasions the family stayed in, Faith and I undertook needlework and played the piano at our mother's encouragement. Winston and Wilfred helped father in the garden, growing fruit, vegetables and flowers. They also played cricket, the guitar, and with some reluctance, the piano.

School holidays were similar to the weekends, which included some days spent away with family members in London and other parts of the country.

My siblings and I experienced a happy and loving childhood. The only time I remember being sad was when Great Uncle Louie died.

Family and friends from Jamaica, America, Canada, and England, and those from Ireland and India who had shared his house, attended the funeral. It was the first one my siblings and I had ever been to.

The cloudy sky threatened rain, which, fortunately, did not arrive.

People sang traditional funeral choruses in harmony in the church, which continued at the graveside. It was a celebratory event. The merriment was transferred to Great Uncle Louie's home, where the attendees congregated with food, beverages, Calypso and Big Band music until late.

No one cried as far as I was aware; however, I did, some weeks later, when I realised I would never again see my Great Uncle Louie or hear his stories about his childhood and when he had first arrived in England in the early 1940s. I will miss his stories, especially about how he had won a lot of money on the Football Pools, and purchasing property with his winnings.

Raised within the love, comfort, and security of my family and our church, I felt unprepared to face the intriguing and hostile world at the age of five. This commenced at primary school in an old Victorian building with its reliable built-in clock.

Kissed and waved off, I was left in the unfamiliar environment of strangers, which is an uncomfortable experience for any child or adult, for that matter.

I wore my brand-new summer uniform, consisting of a blue and white gingham dress, a royal blue cardigan, white socks, black shoes, and a brown satchel. I looked forward to developing my reading, writing and arithmetic skills, which had been introduced to me by my parents for as long as I could remember.

The sound of the handbell rang, inviting the children into the school. My classmates and I sat in the bright and colourful classroom, decorated with pictures relating to the alphabet, numbers and transportation: a red bus, a yellow car, a blue plane, and a green train.

After introductions, painting, and cutting out and pasting shapes onto large thick paper, it was milk time.

The milk, contained in quarter-pint glass bottles secured with silver foil and pierced with a straw, was horrid as it was warm and thick. Unlike at home, it was not kept cool by being placed in a bowl of cold water. After the ordeal of having to drink every drop had ended, we played outside with those from other classrooms.

The following week at playtime, an older white boy with puppy fat called out, 'Blacky!' He then pushed me to the ground and proceeded to run his toy car through the partings of my plaited hair whilst making engine sounds. Some of my peers found this amusing, which seemed to have given the boy permission to continue longer than he might have. This was followed by him saying, 'Wog-a-matter?' in a mock-sympathetic tone in response to my cries, which brought no rescue or comfort from the on-looking playground supervisor. This left me feeling frightened and sad.

Two days later, at dinner, when my siblings and I were given the opportunity to share our day, I told my parents about the incident, and I was gracefully encouraged to defend myself in any way I felt comfortable.

The same boy bullied me almost every day I attended school; his mistreatment included hair-pulling, punching, kicking and name-calling.

I remembered my father's advice to counter the experience, but I was not brave enough. Luckily, neither parent asked about the incident again, nor did I mention it. I only wanted my parents involved when required, at Sports Day and other school events.

In the classroom, inside play followed outside play—stacking bricks, colouring pictures, dressing up, Story Time—and then it was home time. This seemingly strange routine continued for some years.

My expectation of utilising my basic writing, reading and arithmetic skills was only met once I commenced junior school.

The same boy continued bullying me until one day when it got too much, I cuffed him. It worked! The boy ran away crying, and I wondered why I had not done it sooner, but then, as the saying goes, 'Nothing happens before its time.'

Although I had become popular with my peers, this was not the case with some of the teachers, who thought me 'naughty', 'rude', or 'insolent', when all I had really done was ask innocent questions, such as, 'Why are there no coloured children and grown-ups who look like me and my family in these books?'

I eventually left primary school for senior school, with the question remaining unanswered.

In 1965, I commenced my carefully chosen religious senior school, where my desire to learn continued, just like some of my counterparts. However, the responses they received from the teachers were more positive, promoting their self-esteem and confidence.

During the English classes I was accused of plagiarising my stories on more than one occasion. It seemed that the teacher found it difficult to accept that I was able to transfer my imagination onto paper.

There was another incident that also had an impact on me. I had proudly drawn and coloured a picture of Jesus and his disciples in a Religious Education (RE) lesson.

As far as I knew, Bethlehem was near Palestine, where there were people of African origin, so I drew and coloured them with complexions according to this understanding.

When we all handed in our exercise books to the teacher, I received no scores and no comments. Instead, there was a red line running diagonally through my picture. In contrast my peers were praised with awards of ticks and stars. This left me feeling hurt and confused as my stories and picture were much better by far.

Even at the age that I was I felt a sense that these incidents were because I was a Black child.

I told my parents about the incidents that evening at dinner. 'Never mind. We think it's a beautiful picture,' my mother reassured, but my father was silent. His facial expression spoke volumes, clearly indicating his unhappiness at the way his daughter had been treated.

My parents were aware of why the incident occurred, but there was never any discussion about it or similar issues. Perhaps they thought my siblings and I were too young to understand. Still, they encouraged us to focus on what mattered and on the people who mattered.

In school, as was the case with all schools in those days, children were placed into Years according to age, from First to Fifth Year and Sixth Form, if they stayed on. At my school, there were four Sets within each of these years. Those considered academically bright were in Sets One and Two, and those considered less so in Sets Three and Four. These considerations were not based on tests or records from previous educational achievements. It was no coincidence that those whose parents were wealthy or in professional careers were in Sets One and Two, and those whose parents were 'working class', foreign, or considered foreign were in Sets Three and Four. I was placed in Set Three.

In Sets One and Two, there were more academic subjects than in Set Three. Those in Set Four spent a lot of time playing sports.

My colleagues and I moved together through the years.

Whilst I was not confident in maths, I accepted that being in Set Three for this was appropriate; I did however, object to remaining in the same Set for all of the other subjects, particularly when I knew I was more academically able than some of those in the Sets above.

At my mother and father's request at a Parents' Evening, there was an agreement between them and various teaching staff, with polite smiles, that I would be moved to the Sets according to my abilities.

This took some time to materialise, so in the Third Year, out of frustration at my potential being restricted, I gathered my belongings and went to the English and biology classes in Set Two. Surprisingly, the teachers facilitating these classes handed me the relevant material and responded accordingly on the occasions I raised my arm to answer questions. At no time did they challenge my presence.

My father later told me that it was possibly because everyone knew I should have been in Set Two, or even Set One, in the first place. This made me realise that the school system was unfair and that it wasn't that I was not a bright child. I felt proud.

With the continued support of my family, I grew more confident when challenging experiences of racism and sexism.

One day the headteacher, during an assembly, referred to a fight that had taken place between two friends (one black and one white) after they'd had a falling out. She said, 'I do not want all of you Black girls fighting the white girls.'

The Head's statement was alarming. Concerned it would only serve to escalate the situation, I went to see her to challenge her statement. I was told not to be impertinent and sent on my way. By now I wasn't surprised by the Head's response to me and felt indifferent. I was pleased that some of the other students, including the white ones, had also approached her. Fortunately, the two girls made up, so the Head's statement did not cause further conflict.

There was also the time when the typing teacher informed the girls in her class (the boys did woodwork), 'Those of you who do not marry and will, therefore, be unsupported by husbands will unfortunately be required to work as secretaries or shop assistants.' Due to this attitude, the Certificate in Secondary Education (CSE) was the only qualification available to the girls, whilst the boys had the added choice of O-levels, enabling a greater number of career opportunities.

Of course, women could vote by then, but it was before the days of equal opportunities and anti-discriminatory practices.

There was another time when the headmistress reminded the school about its full uniform (the teachers seemed to have one of their own: tweed suits with twin sets and pearls. The younger ones wore knee-length dresses and skirts accompanied by Bri–Nylon blouses and light makeup.

The only two male teachers wore tweed or corduroy jackets and trousers, a shirt, a V-neck pullover and a tie).

The children's uniforms consisted of a black pleated skirt—black trousers for the boys—and a white blouse or shirt. The boys' uniforms required black socks. The younger girls wore white socks, and the older ones wore white or 'flesh-coloured' tights, In those days, white, black, and American tan (also known as 'flesh coloured') were the only tights available—no shades of brown tights existed then. One morning, I was ordered out of the classroom to the headmistress's office for wearing a pair of black tights. When questioned about it, I innocently reminded the headmistress that she had given instructions that white or 'flesh-coloured' tights were to be worn as part of the uniform.

In response, I was told I was being 'downright impertinent' and given detention, where I would be required to 'do lines'. This involved writing several times over, 'I must not be impertinent.' I suppose I was trying to make a point that Black students were also visible. I felt empowered.

This experience—and many others—made me become defiant, as it felt like everything I did was wrong in the eyes of most of the teaching staff. I concluded that I had nothing to lose and continued to challenge, usually by calmly asking questions.

My siblings—who were in their respective school years below me—had their fair share of challenges but given their temperaments and being a little more relaxed, appeared to take things in their stride. One could argue I had paved the way to make that possible.

As well as ensuring that we were unconditionally loved and happy, education in preparation for a good career and quality of life was a priority for my parents.

'"Coloured" children need to work twice as hard to get on in life,' my mother told us in an untypically stern tone after switching off the

TV. The only time we were allowed to watch it was when the news and educational programmes were on, and only after we had completed our homework, followed by an hour of study.

There were plenty of books in our home, and we were allowed to attend the local library, collecting and returning up to four books at a time.

I attended the Monday evening church club, where me and my siblings undertook Bible study, learnt needlecraft, and played musical instruments and various sports. We particularly enjoyed athletics, sometimes competing with each other, with Winston and Faith usually being the winners.

I left school at sixteen with several CSE passes to attend the semi-adult world of college, where I obtained four A-levels in English, maths, biology and science, subjects suitable for a career in nursing.

College life was easier as *all* of the students were encouraged, with the reminder that they had made the decision to further educate themselves. They were neither shouted at nor given detention.

This environment of acceptance and respect contributed to the successful outcomes of many, including me.

By that time, I was allowed to watch 'The Walton's' and 'Top of the Pops', with the Jackson Five, The Supremes, Marvin Gaye, and Stevie Wonder being my favourites. Discos, wearing makeup, or having boyfriends were forbidden, unlike some of my white friends.

I was at the age where my peers were more important than the adults in my life. This caused disagreements between my parents and me, to the point at which I was convinced they were cruel and wanted me unhappy. Up to then, I had embraced without question, my Caribbean and English cultures acquired through the influence of my family, my church and the schools. Though they had once been compatible, they were suddenly in conflict with each other, like the time a white and mixed-parentage school friends called Gillian and Pauline had worn miniskirts and makeup while visiting to ask me to go to the disco with them. We were about fifteen at the time. My parents told me in no uncertain terms that I could not go, and I was sent to my room to study. Luckily, I was not rebellious at home, so I stayed put rather than defy them.

At a school reunion some years later, I accepted that my parents were correct in retaining their principles and boundaries. By then, I recognised it had been out of love and responsibility, as I and others with similar family standards had gone on to higher education with lasting careers and relationships, whilst many of those who did otherwise seemed to struggle with life.

Gillian and Pauline—who had both left school to work in a lingerie factory—were at the reunion. What was striking was that many of those in the higher Sets at school had become 'housewives'. Some worked as secretaries and sales assistants, whilst those who were in the lower Sets went on to further education to become professionals such as nurses, teachers, accountants, probation officers and counsellors. This was despite the school Careers Officer's insistence that some of my British-Caribbean friends and I could only be employed as cleaners or work in offices, shops and factories. This again reinforced my belief that the school system was unfair and was reminded of the reason why our parents had told us about having to work harder than our white counterparts to get on in life.

2

THE TASTE OF INDEPENDENCE

'It is better to protest than to accept injustice.'

Rosa Parks

Just like the other women in my family, nursing was my vocation. I had always wanted to be a nurse and had read some of my mother's textbooks and nursing journals and had discussed these with her.

With a mixture of excitement at being independent, I moved into the nursing accommodation in London. I maintained regular telephone contact with my family, occasionally visiting during my time off.

Whilst training, most of my contributions were received in a patronising manner or dismissed. Initially I was disillusioned by the attitudes of some of the tutors and students. To combat this, I was reminded about my experience at school and how I overcame it. I also recalled and implemented my parents' advice, that of focusing on what mattered despite the obstacles.

My assignments and exam grades were lower than they should have been. However, this did not deter me as I was confident in my abilities.

Bernadette—known as Bernie—was an Irish student nurse. I was sitting alone in the hospital canteen one day when Bernie asked if she could share the table. We soon got talking about how we had always wanted to be nurses and how we were both homesick. We've remained friends ever since.

Bernie knew she did not deserve her higher-assigned grades. Observing the blatant discrimination, although it was in her favour, she tearfully implored, 'It's not fair. You need to say something.'

Knowing it would have been a waste of time and relieved that although the grades were low, they were passes, I casually told Bernie, 'Welcome to my world.' My parents had drilled into me that education was important, and it was something no one could take away from me.

On another occasion, John, a fellow student, said to a group of African and Asian students, 'People like you shouldn't be here. The education, health, legal and other services are for *our* people, so stop complaining about the patients, who shouldn't be here either, not being treated right.'

The hospital staff and a few patients were multicultural, and John seemed threatened by it.

It turned out that John's mother was Jewish. He masked this by being anti-Semitic and racist in fear of being 'found out'.

Whilst I obviously did not agree with John's views, I was comfortable with his brutal honesty. It meant that I knew where I stood with him, and I much preferred that to people who patronised those who were not like themselves - People who eventually said exactly what they truly felt when they did not get their way or when angry. And when exposed, they make excuses for their behaviour by stating, 'It's only friendly banter,' or 'You've just got a chip on your shoulder,' or 'I've got friends who are…' - The same ones who used the institutionally racist and sexist systems to their advantage when it suited them.

Rather than crying and leaving the course—as Jaswinder, a British-born Asian, had due to John's rantings—I used it to become more determined to complete my training so I could support and protect patients and others from so-called 'caring professionals' with views similar to John's.

Though I enjoyed my new career, I soon came to realise that being a nurse was nothing like it was portrayed in books and films. Racism, sexism and discrimination were rife, with some people believing they were better than others and more entitled to being in the world and all it had to offer. Some of the staff and I were falsely accused of not working hard enough despite having a higher volume of work. Some of those 'caring professionals' had also warned us not to 'bite the hand that feeds', which was a veiled threat for us to keep quiet and 'tow-the-line'.

We continued to challenge these injustices. For example, by refusing to take on even more work, and supporting patients and other staff who shared their experiences of discrimination. This sometimes invited positive changes despite our being labelled as 'troublemakers' and accused of 'rocking the boat'.

There was a period in which I went through a particularly difficult time at work when Bertha, an African-born nurse, joined the team. Whilst staunchly religious, sociable and entertaining, she was also brash, judgmental and rarely punctual, and her ability to comprehend was questionable. In short, she was incompetent!

For some reason, Bertha and a couple of other colleagues had taken a dislike to me, who, in comparison, was quiet, polite and reliable but considered a snob who 'acted as if she was white'. (Which suggests that only white people could have these qualities). I was also called a 'nigger' and a 'coconut' by Bertha, even in the presence of known racists.

Racists, some of those of African heritage and others who internalise racism usually view people like me with suspicion. This was because people like me did not fit the negative racial stereotypes held by the perpetrators.

I remained professional throughout the period during which I was harassed, and because I did not rise to it in the way Bertha had hoped, she decided to up the ante.

One afternoon, Bertha followed me into the washroom, and with her heavy body and halitosis, pushed me up against the sink, threatening to ensure I would lose my job.

We were face to face, I made no attempt to free myself. Instead, I looked directly into Bertha's eyes and calmly told her, 'Don't assume you can handle me.'

After observing the sudden fear on Bertha's face as she backed away, I left the washroom, and in doing so, passed a line of Bertha's posse. It was then I realised that she had planned her actions.

I resumed my nursing duties, whilst Bertha loudly boasted about how she had 'put me in my place' to the encouragement and cackling of her listeners.

A week and a half later, Miss Jones, the buxom, unsmiling senior nurse, called me into her office. She commenced by stating that she had always admired my professionalism and was disappointed about information that had been brought to her attention by some colleagues of mine.

Miss Jones requested an explanation regarding some confidential documents that had gone missing and informed me that they had been found in my locker.

Astonished but composed, I denied taking the documents in question, suspecting that Bertha had something to do with it. However, I refrained from informing Miss Jones about the threats and racist remarks Bertha had made, as Miss Jones who was white, may not have understood.

Bertha got away with bullying others besides me. Given that she was overtly religious, friendly, always cheerful and had told on 'troublemakers', the assumption was that it was not in her nature to be so cruel and deceptive.

As it looked as if I might be in some serious trouble, I sought out Victor's advice. Victor was a friend also of Jamaican parentage, whom I'd met at college and with whom I occasionally socialised. He was an accountant, which was unusual in those days.

Victor had also experienced workplace harassment. He left his place of work, and became self-employed, representing those in need of independent professional support.

At a meeting held with Miss Jones, Victor, Bertha, and myself the following week, Bertha defused the initial tense atmosphere with her usual buffoonish behaviour. The forty-five-minute meeting ended with Miss Jones concluding that there appeared to be a 'clash of personalities', and she hoped Bertha, and I could work professionally in the best interest of the patients, staff and all concerned.

The outcome of the meeting left me feeling frustrated as the real issues had not been resolved, despite Victor's support.

As those who had attended the meeting departed to resume their respective duties, Bertha gave me a sneaky look and grin.

Poor Bertha thought she was immune. She had not realised that some of the colleagues she 'entertained' berated her with reference to her colour, size, various ill-fitting wigs, and incompetence behind her back.

I resolved to play the waiting game, knowing it would only be a matter of time before the 'masters' would 'whip' Bertha's back.

In the meantime, I survived working with the psychopaths and their toxic relationships by turning to my faith. I also recalled my parents' advice to focus on what mattered and the people who mattered despite any obstacles I might encounter.

Some years later, I learned that Bertha had been sacked on the spot for theft.

3

THE AWAKENING

'The only protection against injustice is power - physical, financial and scientific.'

Marcus Mosiah Garvey

*L*ike many other students, I became someone with perspectives and opinions of my own about how the world ought to be—without greed, hunger, exploitation, inequality, discrimination and other negatives. News of suffering through wars and famine, whilst those in other countries wasted food and lived lavish lifestyles, upset and frustrated me.

In my spare time, I did voluntary work at HeadStart, a Pan-African bookshop on Tottenham's West Green Road, which sold books and African, Caribbean and South American art and crafts. All of this was tastefully displayed, attracting many who admired and purchased the items.

I read some books, and in the record department, situated in the shop's basement, heard songs about continued global injustices and discrimination experienced by people of African heritage wherever they lived in the world.

Aside from the bookshop, I attended meetings and rallies protesting the South African apartheid system and supporting the liberation of Africa. I also, with others challenged the use of banned medication and other products introduced to people in what was called the 'Third World.'

The bookshop was a centre for the knowledge of Africa, providing awareness of aspiration, equality, peace and justice. Knowledge not found in mainstream newspapers or taught in mainstream education.

Spending time in the bookshop and attending its Sunday afternoon meetings encouraging discussion awoke my interest in Africa. I questioned why a continent so rich in natural minerals and resources was unable to sustain many of its people while sustaining those living elsewhere. I wondered why there was constant wars and famine, presented to myself and the rest of society with depictions of starving children and helpless parents who were only able to obtain food, water and medicine with European assistance.

Did these images contribute to how most people of African heritage—whatever their position, gender, age, culture, religion or class and wherever they lived—seemed disrespected and exploited by non-Africans at every opportunity, including those who had also experienced oppression? I also wondered how these images contributed to why some Africans, including African descendants, internalised a mentality of self-hate and dependency.

If other nations were dependent upon Africans and African resources for their development and sustenance, why did it seem as if some Africans were unable to utilise Africa's God-given resources to meet their own needs? In other words, why 'swap' food with its natural pharmaceutical properties—including gold, diamonds, copper, uranium, rubber, iron and other natural gifts—for other people's cast-offs and call it aid?

I was a member of the 1970s 'Rebel Generation', that stood up against injustice, including police brutality. I also read many books about those who had the same concerns and had devised solutions.

One, in particular, was about a man of African descent, born in Jamaica, called Marcus Mosiah Garvey (1887-1940). He was a political activist, publisher, journalist and entrepreneur who mobilised millions of other Africans within and outside of the continent of Africa. Garvey encouraged them to accept Africa as their homeland and consider themselves Africans, whether or not they were born or lived there. He also advocated for the peaceful liberation of Africa.

Marcus Garvey reminded people that they'd had a rich and glorious history before enslavement, and therefore, had reasons to be proud. They were also able to regain and control their own destinies, be self-governing and support their freedom, thus lessening the risk of discrimination and exploitation.

Along with his family and friends, Marcus Garvey founded the Universal Negro Improvement Association (UNIA), with branches in Africa, the Caribbean, and the Americas.

The UNIA owned a shipping company called The Black Star Line. It also founded the first political party in Jamaica in 1929, called the People's Political Party, giving people a voice. It also influenced the development of agricultural industries, the University of West Indies in Jamaica, the Black Cross Nurses, the Youth Brigade, and other institutions aimed at improving the situation of Africans in Jamaica and other parts of the Caribbean, Africa and elsewhere in the world.

I concluded that the UNIA proved that people of African heritage in Africa and elsewhere in the world could continue to motivate themselves through self-belief and by working together. Though the legacy of the African holocaust sometimes made this difficult, it was essential to focus on achieving change towards self-reliance, progress and respect.

My understanding of Marcus Garvey's philosophies was illustrated in my observation of nations identifying with their original homelands no matter where they lived in the world. These people retained their languages, traditions and cultures as part of their identity, no matter where their homeland was.

These nations took responsibility for themselves and their interests. They also strived to improve the future for their children and grandchildren, with the cycle repeating from generation to generation. They were also respectfully known according to their land of origin—Asians, Europeans, Mediterraneans and so on, and did not describe themselves or accept being described by others according to their skin colour, which negated them as holistic human beings.

As far as I was concerned, people of African heritage, born and living in Africa, the Caribbean, Britain, America, Europe and elsewhere in the world, were entitled to the same. To be a psychologically free, self-governing people, respectfully recognised according to their countries of origin, wherever they lived in the world. I believed this would prevent the patronisation and exploitation of Africa, Africans and their descendants, and therefore, change the physical and psychological global images of them being an impoverished and dependent people.

Though I recognised that the situation was much more complex, I still believed this to be a solution and of utmost importance towards improving the world. I ignored accusations of terrorism and racism by racists in their various guises. I also ignored accusations of terrorism and racism by those who had consciously and unconsciously internalised racism - those who believed the myth of (Black) African inferiority and the need to be ruled and dominated by others.

I had formed lifelong friendships with likeminded people from the bookshop—namely Victor, Andrew, a probation officer; Maureen, who was a teacher; and Ursula, a social worker—with whom I attended the annual African Liberation Rallies on May bank holidays, amongst other political and social events.

4

THE MEETING

At one of these rallies, dignitaries spoke about the current state of Africa and the need for its liberation. There were pleas for much needed change, which could be achieved by anyone who cared. The atmosphere was charged. There were chants of – 'We want change. We want it now!'

As the crowd marched and chanted, a skinny young man who spoke with a South London accent said, 'Hi, I'm Michael, and you're my queen.' He added, 'We're going to be married.' It never occurred to him that I might be in a relationship with one of the men I was with.

Initially, I didn't think he was talking to me, partly because his voice was nearly inaudible against the background of the chanting crowd, drums and whistles, so I didn't respond and carried on walking.

Michael repeated himself. This time, he was closer, and we made eye contact. I was wearing platform shoes, so our eyes were on the same level. He smiled, revealing even white teeth surrounded by a slim face partly covered with hair. The weather was damp and dull, yet he wore sunglasses. He removed them, revealing large, dark brown eyes canopied by thick black lashes. He had an afro and wore bell bottoms, which swung around his long legs. Though I also wore my hair in an afro and looked slim in my long, African print dress, I preferred my men to be a little more filled out.

I smiled at him, wishing he'd go away as I didn't think he was committed to the reasons for the rally.

Michael asked for my name and telephone number. This was followed by him serenading me with a chorus of 'Queen Majesty' (by the Techniques).

Can't you see I'm not interested? I thought, but I smiled nevertheless and said, 'I'm Gloria.' It was the first name that came to mind, I didn't know why.

'A beautiful name for a beautiful lady.' Michael beamed smarmily before asking me out.

He just wasn't getting the message.

'I don't live locally,' I said in desperation.

'Where you are, there I am.' His persistence seemed unshakable, so I stopped in my tracks, found an envelope in my bag, emptied its contents, and wrote a false telephone number on it. I handed it to Michael—who seemed beyond grateful—and caught up and continued walking with the group I'd accompanied to the rally.

The rally ended with some people signing up to various organisations, all with the aim of working towards improving the conditions of African people and their descendants around the world.

Within five years of qualifying, I was a fully competent nurse who had been promoted to staff nurse. As usual, my staff and I worked at full capacity.

According to the government and the hospital, there were insufficient funds to employ extra staff. This, of course, placed a strain on the existing nurses, who, understandably, did not want to read about themselves in the newspapers for making mistakes due to work overload.

I'd had a particularly difficult day, having to challenge a student nurse who believed she needed no training or guidance. She seemed to be under the absurd impression that nursing was a simple matter of making beds, giving patients medication, serving meals and emptying bedpans.

Due to the way the training was carried out, the student had completed the minimum requirements for passing her first placement. I could only hope that once this particular student had finished her training, her knowledge and attitude would improve. Fortunately, other students I'd supported in the past were appropriate—I'd verified their suitability to practice as nurses at the end of their final placements, and rightly so.

That night, I was to attend the Bob Marley and the Wailers concert at the Regal in Edmonton, north London, with my boyfriend, Carl. I left the day behind me as I got ready. I initially met Carlton—known as Carl—at a bus stop, where we got talking about the wet weather and the length of time it was taking for the bus to arrive.

We enjoyed our time together, attending Club Norik, All Nations and Shady Grove, following the competing heavy bass sound systems. Going to the nightclubs was like going to church and being reminded, through spiritual Roots and Culture music, that there would soon be deliverance, peace and unity. However, unlike churches, they were dark, hot, smoky and full to capacity.

Carl, an electrician who lived with his parents in Chiswick, west London, worked hard. He hated being an employee and planned to work for himself one day.

Not unlike many other parents, my mother and father would have preferred Carl to be a doctor or a lawyer, and his parents would have preferred that I was interested in being a stay-at-home wife and mother. Although unspoken, it may have been these underlying expectations that had put a strain on our relationship, and we went our separate ways after three years. As we still cared for each other, this was a mutual separation and for the next three years we kept in touch via letters.

Deciding that I was better off having friends than a partner, I spent much of my time nursing, volunteering at the bookshop, socialising occasionally, and visiting relatives and friends during my time off.

Accomplish What You Will

Some years later, I heard that Carl was married with four children and living in Canada, where he owned a successful company.

Two years later, in a job I loved and to which I was committed, although busy, it was manageable.

Following a staff meeting in the month of February, there was a sudden surge in activity.

'Nurse, come quickly,' said Dr Choy, who was about to utilise his stethoscope.

Without hesitation, I walked quickly and carefully through the light, airy corridor of St Luke's, with its polished yet non-slippery floor with some of my staff following me. There had been a traffic accident, and a number of people had to be admitted. Some of the injured were trolleyed onto the wards, with their rows of single beds and lockers with gifts of flowers, grapes, Lucozade, and 'get well' cards against a background of the usual 'hospital aroma'.

It seemed that a lorry driver had a heart attack, causing the incident, and he was admitted directly to the theatre.

A woman was hysterical. She had not been injured, but the man she was with was unconscious. 'Do something!' she ordered.

'We're doing the best we can. He's stable now,' I consoled.

'Is he going to die? It's all my fault. He didn't want to drive. We should've taken the train as planned.' The ample woman's body shook as she sobbed.

I extended a box of tissues and offered the woman some tea.

Mopping her flowing eyes, the woman continued, 'If he dies, I'll die too. Oh no, why—'

'Please, try to keep calm,' I interrupted. 'What's your name?'

'Melanie,' the woman replied, dabbing her face and blowing her nose.

'I'll see that your husband's well looked after.'

'Oh, Tiny's not my husband; he's my little brother. I've always looked out for him since we were children after our parents died. It's just the two of us here. The rest of our family's in Ghana.'

I thought. *Poor woman. What a responsibility. I feel so sorry for her.* I informed Melanie that I would check on the other patients and then return.

Within two hours, the atmosphere at St Luke's resumed its manageable busyness, with the injured and the shocked sedated.

Melanie appeared to be in a daze. She jumped slightly in response to my touch on her shoulder in an attempt to comfort her. 'He looks so peaceful,' she eventually said.

As promised, I looked after Tiny, who was in a coma - washing and shaving him and changing his bedclothes. I also took his temperature and checked his pulse and blood pressure, speaking to him softly all the while, telling him about the tasks I was about to perform and praising him afterwards.

I also described the weather and carried on one-sided conversations with him. On one occasion, I asked him why he was called Tiny when, clearly, he was not.

Due to the distance from the hospital to her home, Melanie visited every other day, bringing clean pyjamas and culturally traditional meals, fruit and drink, always in the hope that Tiny would soon be awake to enjoy them.

5

THE RETURN HOME

'Home is where the heart is.'

Gaius Plinius Secundus (Pliny the Elder)

*I*t was 1980, the afternoon before my parents would take off before emigrating to Jamaica. My siblings and I were spending some time with them. It was always the plan that they would return after they had retired, and we had grown and left home.

The reunion included family and friends. It was a sad yet celebratory affair. There was plenty of food, which included curry goat, rice, salad, drinks, a range of music, laughter and shared photographs, including those of the house in Ocho Rios – an area in the parish of St Ann, where my parents would be living.

Being organised, my parents had already packed and updated their passports, ready for their 'big day'. It would be a new chapter for them. They had worked hard and paid off the mortgage on the house they planned to rent, and now they were going to spend some time together. It was something they had not really done since we were born.

The following morning was mayhem. My siblings and I squabbled over who should use the bathroom first, which our parents seemed to find amusing as it brought back memories of when we were young.

The arranged minibus arrived at seven o' clock in the morning to take my parents, siblings and me to Heathrow Airport in London.

The airport was bustling with staff and passengers coming and going, all of them carrying suitcases, bags and trollies.

At last, it was time for my parents to board the plane, a Boeing 747.

The family exchanged hugs, kisses, tears and waves.

As the plane lifted to the sky, the bustle of the airport suddenly quietened, with those within it seeming to move in slow motion.

Those of us who had accompanied my parents to the airport returned to their respective places of residence; there was no need for them to go back to the family home in Maidstone.

Each of us had promised our parents that we'd maintain contact, support each other, and visit them in Jamaica, and we kept our promises. We met up for birthdays and holidays as singles, then with our respective spouses, then with our children and later, our grandchildren. For example, at Christmas in the same year, we gathered at Winston and his girlfriend, Shola's home in Wandsworth, southwest London.

Everyone managed to fit at the long dining table, with a large stuffed turkey at its centre. As well as roast potatoes, and vegetables. There was jollof rice, rice and peas, stewed chicken, plantain, and more, some of which were contributed by those in attendance.

After lunch, we exchanged phone calls with relatives living near and far, including our parents and other relatives in Jamaica, America and elsewhere. Wilfred then played the piano whilst the rest of us gathered to sing Christmas carols and other favourites.

It was coming to the end of March 1981, and I was required to take my annual leave before the new financial year. My break from work was well-deserved and overdue. Somehow, the number of responsibilities that had come with the staff shortages had prevented me from finding the time to arrange a holiday.

I was excited about the prospect of seeing my parents again.

The direct flight from Heathrow to Montego Bay Airport gave me the opportunity to relax, read half of 'A Woman of Substance', a rags-to-riches novel by Barbara Taylor-Bradford. I then snoozed, then watched a film, and consumed the unappetising cuisine served on plastic trays.

I stepped off the plane for my fourth visit, absorbing the physical and spiritual warmth and tropical sounds of the alternative environment. I retrieved my cases at a leisurely pace and entered a waiting taxi, tipping the driver when I arrived at my destination.

I ignored the mosquitoes' welcome and dabbed at my damp face.

The air became more bearable, with the presence of the tall evergreen trees and other vegetation surrounding my parents' four-bedroom detached home in the secluded area in Ocho Rios.

It had been a while since I'd last seen my parents, but I'd maintained weekly telephone contact with them. When they saw me, they greeted me lovingly.

The first time I had been to Jamaica was with my parents and siblings. I was ten at the time, Winston was nine, Faith was eight, and Wilfred was seven. We alternated lodgings between our paternal and maternal grandparents and visited other family members, who took us sightseeing and shopping. This included going to the Dunns River Falls, the National Heroes Park, Harbour View, and other places of interest.

I was struck by the number of relatives I had, and how most of them were self-sufficient.

The previous generations had built their own detached homes, surrounded by fertile land with cows, goats, chickens, many fruits and even coffee trees and a range of vegetables, all of which had been handed down from generation to generation. Also, the main houses contained the tombs of those who had gone before.

My parents had aged, though they looked strikingly similar to each other. I supposed that it was inevitable, as they had known each other since they were children and had been married at eighteen and seventeen.

They were self-sufficient, growing their own fruit, vegetables, beans and rearing chickens and goats like the previous generations.

A lot had changed since the first time I'd gone to Jamaica. Some of the older people had passed away, and there was tap water and electricity in most rural areas.

My parents and other family members all asked when I might settle down, which meant being married with children. Until then, I thought I was settled. I had a career and hobbies I enjoyed and could not envisage there could ever be the time and space for anything or anyone else.

It was the fourth week of my six-week holiday, and I already felt the dread of returning to England, thinking about how my now seemingly boring life was likely to resume as usual. I would continue to share the same three-bedroom house with Victor and Bernie in which I'd lived since leaving the nursing accommodations.

I'd always thought of myself as being free-spirited, avoiding inhibitions, however, I made a detailed list of what I wanted to achieve within the next five years.

The list included a description of the man I wanted in my life once I realised that the potential for being married was a reality after all.

The night before returning to England, I dreamt of meeting the man I described. He was medium built, strong, and regal-like, but just as I was about to see his face, the cockerel crowed at its usual time of five thirty, waking me.

Part Two

SOUL TO SOUL

Love is patient and kind... Love never gives up and its faith, hope and patience never fail'

1 Corinthian 13:4&7

Besides being a nurse, I was also interested in education, so I attended a conference with Victor, Andrew, Maureen, and Ursula. The conference was titled - 'Is the Education System Failing Black Children?' organised by a Methodist church in southwest London.

This was amidst concerns for the number of children of African descent underachieving in mainstream education in comparison with their non-African counterparts. It resulted in a very small number of children succeeding in higher education and professional careers. Some had their confidence eroded by some teachers and even some parents, who were unable to believe they could be self-employed and positively make their way in the world.

During the fifteen-minute break, someone called, 'Nurse! Nurse Walker—I thought it was you. Do you remember us from St Luke's hospital?' Melanie approached me and introduced her brother, 'Tiny', who appeared quite different upright as he looked well and was taller than I'd imagined.

'We came to see you to thank you for everything, but you were on holiday,' Melanie continued.

'No need. I was just doing my job,' I responded, slightly embarrassed.

'Tiny, stop it! She's beautiful, but you don't need to stare,' Melanie said, playfully tapping her brother. 'You wouldn't think he was a university lecturer,' she continued.

I shook Tiny's hand, noting a slight sadness in his eyes just before he looked away. I felt concerned but didn't show it.

It was time for the conference to resume. Melanie suggested we all sat together, but I informed her I was with friends on the other side of the hall. I did, however, agree to Melanie's suggestion of meeting up afterwards.

Due to the number of people present at the event, I wasn't able to see Melanie and Tiny before leaving the venue that evening.

The overwhelming success of this and other such events and the petitions that followed contributed to new policies and procedures. For example, making it illegal to discriminate against people who were different from those considered 'mainstream' in terms of their physical, personal, social, economic and other backgrounds. Some of this later influenced The Equalities Act of 2010.

Eight months later, there was an annual fundraising dinner, a 'Black Tie and Gown' event. The purpose of the gala was to raise funds for a school in the rural areas of Akosombo near Accra in Ghana and one in Browns Town in the parish of St Ann in Jamaica.

Much to my surprise I saw Tiny at the event and approached him. He was reserved when he acknowledged me but briefly managed to explain that he had organised the event. Again, I saw sadness in his eyes. Unsure of what to make of it, I made my excuses and refocused on the stage performances.

Later, Tiny gave a keynote address to the audience. He was striking in his black-tie attire as he spoke, and I was un-patronisingly impressed with his passion and eloquence regarding the reasons for the event, which was to ensure that all children had access to education and opportunities towards improving their futures.

Following the meal, much to my surprise, Tiny asked me to dance to the Lovers' Rock and R'n'B music. He held me close enough to smell his unique scent and feel his heart beating.

Each time the music stopped; he held me close when I expected him to let me go to dance with someone else.

The sparkling, rotating ceiling ball cast speckles of white light on silhouettes of swaying couples and over the dark hall. I decided to embrace the moment, only fleetingly thinking about the effect our combined perspiration would have on my recently hot-combed hairstyle.

I surprised myself when I agreed to go on a date with Tiny when he asked. We attended the Harlem Ballet Company's performance at the Sadler's Wells Theatre in Islington, London, in addition to nightclubs, where we danced and drank Babycham and Cherry B. We also visited various restaurants. Given that we both enjoyed martial arts, we attended late-night cinema screenings at the Rio in Hackney, playfully mimicking kung fu moves to the tune of 'Kung Fu Fighting' in our moments alone.

Tiny had received his nickname due to his size when he was six and Melanie was ten.

Following the death of their parents and not having any other family in England, Tiny and Melanie lived with foster carers, Mr and Mrs Edwards, in Croydon, southeast London.

Mr Edwards was plump and reserved. Mrs Edwards was also plump; however, she talked and laughed a lot. They were both from Dominica.

The couple had no children of their own. After three miscarriages—which they later believed was a blessing in disguise—they fostered about a hundred children over thirty years, and they had the photographs to verify it.

Mr Edwards was a carpenter by trade until he retired.

Mrs Edwards was a childminder until she saw an advertisement about recruiting foster carers on the TV. She and Mr Edwards attended an open session at their local town hall to obtain further information. They applied, and within three months, were assessed and approved as foster carers.

The couple embraced looking after the children and young people to the best of their abilities, which included taking them on holidays and spending time at the villa they owned in Anguilla.

Tiny was passionate about all children and young people experiencing a safe and secure environment in which they could grow, learn and develop, through education and life skills to enable life choices as he had with Mr and Mrs Edwards. It was an experience his foster brother and best friend, Brady, only enjoyed once he'd joined the family at the age of twelve, although he had been in the care system since he was four.

I enjoyed my time with Tiny; however, there was something about him that I could not quite put my finger on. However, we continued to date.

A month and a half into our relationship, Tiny walked me to the door of the house I shared with friends Bernie and Victor. Whilst looking deep into my eyes, he said, 'You're my queen.'

I smiled, attempting to contain the laughter threatening to burst from inside of me and told him, 'Someone said that to me some years ago.'

The sadness in his eyes I had seen before returned. Tiny frowned and said, 'It was me.' He paused. 'I also said we were going to be married.'

Shocked, I stared at him in disbelief for some seconds. My heart suddenly started pounding.

'When I saw you again at the education conference, I thought you didn't want to know me. You'd made it clear before, the day you said your name was Gloria and gave me a non-existent phone number,' Tiny continued.

I remained silent, recalling both events before saying, 'But at the hospital—'

'Remember, I came out of the coma when you were on holiday'

I stared at him, wide-eyed and speechless.

He pulled me gently towards him. I felt his heart beating as he must have felt mine, and he told me he loved me. My eyes filled with tears in response, eventually spilling over.

Tiny brushed the tears from my cheeks before kissing them.

Alone that night, I reflected on each time I'd met Tiny, whose real name was Michael.

Michael, that lanky young man with baggy bell bottoms, was now masculine, clean-shaven, and sophisticated. His hair was cut very low. I recalled the sadness I'd first noticed when Tiny's—Michael's—sister, Melanie, had introduced us at the conference, and I cried myself to sleep that night after realising how much I must have hurt him, even though it was unwittingly.

Tiny agreed to let me call him by his proper name—which we both preferred anyway—and we continued to date. This included going to museums and art galleries, also on boat trips and attending social and political gatherings. Some of these gatherings followed a spate of deaths of people in the community due to racist attacks and police brutality, at which the victims' families pleaded with those in attendance, who were enraged, not to retaliate.

Michael and Brady were imprisoned for ten days—'for rioting', according to the police—when all they had done was to march peacefully with others through the streets of Brixton in south London.

This was in protest to the killing and mistreatment of members of the African and Caribbean communities.

A scuffle ensued, and the police, who seemed to be spoiling for a fight, started beating with batons, anyone they could get hold of, arresting some of them, including Michael and Brady.

The peaceful march turned into an uprising lasting three days.

6

THE WEDDINGS

*M*ichael and I didn't initially plan to get married. We were happy just living together until we succumbed to pressure from our families. Faith, who followed the family tradition of becoming a nurse, was the first to get married to Bentley, a property investor.

It was the Autum of 1982 when Winston, Faith, Wilfred, me, and our partners met at our childhood house in Maidstone, as we usually did on special occasions. 'I have something to tell you all,' Faith said, fostering intrigue in our minds as we sat around the dining table, following a delicious three-course meal.

'Bentley and I are getting married next month,' she continued. 'We're not having a big wedding. It will be at the registry office.'

My mother, who was on a two-week visit from Jamaica, hugged Faith and Bentley whilst saying, 'My baby's getting married.'

Everyone was happy with the news except for protective big brother Winston. 'Why so quickly? You hardly know each other,' he said.

'We met a year ago at a property seminar and again ten months later, and we have been dating ever since,' Faith informed.

'My intentions are honourable,' Bentley added reassuringly.

My father, who was also visiting from Jamaica, shook Bentley's hand and invited us all to make a toast, indicating approval. That was enough for Winston to also welcome Bentley into our family.

My mother wondered if Faith was in the 'family way' but she did not question it. She was, however, proven correct when Bentley Junior arrived seven months after the wedding.

A year later, Winston married Shola, and a year after that, Wilfred married Paulette. Even Michael's foster brother, Brady—who was known as Muhammad following his conversion to Islam—married Nia, his childhood sweetheart. She had also been fostered by Mr and Mrs Edwards for six months until returning to live with her father.

In 1985, when Michael and I were in our mid-twenties, we decided that we would also get married.

Faith, friends Bernie, Ursula, Maureen, and Michael's sister, Melanie, were the main organisers.

Michael later told me the story of his groom's party. About when he, Andrew, Mohammad, Bentley, and Victor were getting ready at Andrew's home. And how Andrew had occasionally turned up the volume when a tune they all knew the words to came on, such as, 'Here I Come' by Denis Brown and 'A Little Way Different' by Errol Dunkley.

'Woyyy!' and 'Ooh,' the men had said whilst dancing around the room.

Michael also shared with me that he had told Mohammad and his other friends that he just wanted a few drinks in the local bar. To which they agreed. Mohammad—who did not indulge in alcohol—drove to the other side of London to the Granaries Night Club in Croydon, where they had more drinks and snacks and the added surprise of Michael being 'wooed' by what he initially thought were two female police officers.

While this was happening, I was at Maureen's home in East London, along with Bernie, Ursula and Melanie, getting ready for my bridal party, which included doing each other's hair and makeup. We each wore black tee-shirts with our names printed on them in gold, except for mine, which had 'The Bride' printed on it.

We sang 'Silly Games' by Janet Kay and 'Paradise' by Jean Adebambo, including the ability to reach the high notes.

'I hope Michael's not going to be left tied to a lamppost by his friends somewhere,' Ursula said, laughing.

'They'd better not!' I replied sternly.

'Whatever they're up to, let's hope it will be sensible, but fun,' said Bernie.

At the Granaries Night Club, on a different floor from our male counterparts, we danced and drank Champagne.

The arranged male stripper group, called 'Satisfaction', was an embarrassing yet fun surprise for me.

Breaking the tradition of the bride not seeing the groom before the 'big day', our parties came together at midnight to dance to the eclectic music.

Leaving the venue at three o'clock in the morning, 'hens' and the 'stags' went our separate ways, each sober enough to prepare for the day ahead.

My parents came from Jamaica, and Michael's aunt and uncle from Ghana attended our wedding at Enfield Baptist Church in north London.

Melanie, my parents, Mohammad (who was the best man), and my siblings and their spouses, along with other family and friends, filled the church.

Bernie and Victor were now a couple; however, Bernie was visiting her sick mother in Ireland, so Victor attended the wedding alone.

Some of the guests wore traditional African garb, while others wore Western attire. I wore a long, white, off-the-shoulder dress that hugged my naturally slim frame. It had gold thread braiding detail around the neckline and hem. I pinned up my long dreadlocks, enabling me to wear the Nefertiti-style crown that matched my dress with the same gold thread detail.

Michael wore a white, knee-length dashiki—a version of my outfit—except the gold thread braiding ran around the neckline and sleeves and down the outer seams of his trousers.

My father, straight-backed and teeth glistening, walked me proudly down the aisle to an unconventional but suitable wedding march whilst nodding at the guests on either side of the aisle.

The service—which was presided over by the now elderly Pastor McHugh, who, it seemed not so long ago, had christened me—lasted approximately forty-five minutes.

It was a beautiful and humorous affair with Muhammad's pretence of losing the rings.

I experienced a sense of déjà-vu as we were about to kiss for the first time as man and wife, suddenly recalling the dream I'd had on my last night in Jamaica five years earlier. It was Michael; I was sure—I could now see his face.

Fortunately, the British end-of-July weather was as it should have been, enhancing the mood and allowing us to take respectable photographs.

The reception at the banqueting suite at Forty Hall in Enfield, north London, was tastefully decorated with purple, yellow and white flowers and balloons.

Each table was covered in white linen, with a miniature centrepiece of the same flowers, disposable cameras, the expected cutlery and white with gold-rimmed crockery.

The three-tiered iced fruitcake was adorned with figurines appropriately representing Micheal and I formed the perfect sculpture.

Our siblings and Muhammad surpassed themselves with hilarious accounts of their lives with us, the newlyweds, leaving many in fits of laughter and streaming eyes.

The children of family and friends performed a show they had secretly organised, and the line dance we led was a memorable addition to the spectacular event.

Mr Michael Mensah and I, now Mrs Patience Walker-Mensah, along with some of those who'd travelled to attend the wedding, remained to experience the famous London Notting Hill Carnival, which was enjoyable. It was colourful in terms of its peoples, costumes, and floats.

There were also steel pans and sound systems playing calypso, jazz, reggae, and soul music.

The aroma of jerk and curried chicken, fried plantain and popcorn filled the air.

Everyone danced as they followed the floats. Even some members of the police force joined in.

On the night before the honeymoon, in early September, there was a small gathering of family and friends at Mohammad and Nia's home in Streatham, south London.

The weather permitted a catered garden party with Caribbean and West African food.

There were drinks and music, and the topics of conversation ranged from how delightful the wedding had been, where people were going for their holidays, and the latest 'must see' films.

Excited children chased each other in between the chattering adults who were standing and milling about.

Michael made a short speech, similar to the one he'd made at our wedding reception: 'My wife and I would like to thank you for coming to join us in celebration of our union. Mind you, we've been together for a while now. Thank you. Cheers.'

Everyone raised their glasses and toasted 'Cheers,' in return.

The honeymoon was in Kumasi, in the Ashanti Region of Ghana, the birthplace of Michael's parents. It was similar to Jamaica, as far as I was concerned. Both had beautiful landscapes and were multicultural, with beautiful peoples from other parts of Africa, the Caribbean and elsewhere.

Many Ghanaians spoke English as well as Akan, Twi and other languages, some of which I was able to recognise as they clearly had some influence on the Jamaican patois.

In the two weeks, we travelled to as many places as possible, taking in as much as possible, spending some of the time with Michael's relatives in rural and city areas.

When I stood on the green hill outside the villa called Shanti Lodge, observing and absorbing the warmth and beauty, I felt free, at peace and content. I thanked the One who had created the beautiful land, also giving thanks that I could be close to those from whom I'd descended generations and generations before.

7

POST HONEYMOON

'Honour the hurt and the pain, then let them go to experience the joy that is set before you.'

TD Jakes

I became pregnant despite being on the contraceptive pill, so we decided to move from our one-bedroom flat on Arthur Street in Islington, north London, the one we'd shared since moving in together four months after dating.

It was a Sunday morning when I felt a twinge. It passed, and I continued to prepare breakfast.

Michael did the washing up whilst I got ready to go shopping before we met Mohammad and Nia for lunch at Mr and Mrs Edwards' home, an event that occurred every other month. The pain returned as we were about to leave the flat. This time, it was severe, so Michael drove me to the local hospital.

During my overnight stay, I was examined and told by the sonographer that I was losing the baby. I was two and a half months pregnant.

The loss was a devastating blow for Micheal and me. We felt sad and helpless.

After the loss of our baby, we focused on raising the finances needed to move home. The preoccupation meant both of us worked overtime. I worked in an older people's residential home via an agency on my days off from St Luke's, and Michael, as well as teaching full-time at Middlesex University, provided home tuition three evenings a week and taught at a supplementary school on Saturday mornings.

I had a 'bottom drawer' housing pots, pans, other kitchen items and bedding, as since we were teenagers, my siblings and I had been encouraged to keep such items for times like this.

The other reason for wanting to move was because our white, neighbours, were nowhere as innocent as they had presented or as many believed them to be. They did not approve of having us living next door to them, and in a 'respectful' way, they were able to influence others in the neighbourhood. This wore on us although, due to work commitments, we spent very little time at home.

As well as the racial abuse, the neighbours called the police on a number of occasions, alleging drug dealing and loud music. They also presented themselves as victims. On some of these occasions, the police were invited into our smoke-free home and introduced to our transistor radio, which, in no way, could have produced the disturbing volume reported. The police appeared to be satisfied with their findings but didn't share how they would deal with the false reports.

The last straw was when I was threatened with a knife. Michael was uncharacteristically enraged and about to inflict bodily harm, the consequences of which would have been detrimental to both parties. However, I managed to calm him down by encouraging him to realise that the neighbours were relying on such a response. They had, after all, mockingly said, 'Ooh'd you fink our boys are gonna believe?' knowing that the police— 'their boys'—would likely perceive Michael as 'an aggressive Black man from whom society needed protection.' This was an unfortunate, commonly held view amongst some members of the constabulary about men of African heritage.

Although the harassment continued, we focused on our respective careers and the extra work we had taken on, and within two years, we had saved enough for a deposit. We moved to a three-bed semi on Hillfield Avenue in leafy Winchmore Hill in north London.

Michael and I arranged our home as planned, with an off-white-coloured walls and wooden floors with Egyptian rugs throughout. The through-lounge was furnished with two caramel-coloured leather sofas and two filled bookcases in alcoves on either side of the fireplace.

On the wall, a framed picture, 'Jazz from the Cellar' by Ernest Watson, hung, featuring a saxophone player in a basement with an audience surrendering to the peace and tranquillity of the music.

Above the sideboard in the dining area was a framed text that read, 'Christ is head of this house, the unseen guest at every meal, the silent listener to every conversation.' The six-seater dining set included four upholstered cream brocade fabric chairs and two carvers. The window and French door curtains were made from Kente fabric as did the cushions, which sat like companions next to the cream brocade ones on the sofas.

Each ensuite bedroom was furnished with the usual essentials, and although there was a fireplace in all of them, only the one in the living room was utilised when we felt a romantic ambience was needed, sometimes along with the central heating on particularly cold evenings.

The beamed ceiling country kitchen was always warm with its glossy green Rayburn.

The back garden, where we held many a barbeque with family and close friends, was small and easily maintained.

8

THE PASSING

I was in a meeting at work when I received the news of my parents' sudden death. It came from a distant relative who resided in Jamaica.

They died whilst driving in one of Jamaica's ferocious storms.

In response to this tragic news, I was numb and as if on autopilot I drove home to telephone my siblings and other relatives. We later met up to arrange an immediate flight out.

In the same month, Michael and I, my siblings, and other relatives flew out, and the funeral was arranged. For nine nights, people came from far and wide to pay their respects, consume food and share hymns and fond memories of my parents.

Following the funeral service, they were laid to rest together in the tomb, along with those who had passed away in the years and generations before, on the plot of land in Charlton, St Ann, which had belonged to the family since their forced arrival from Africa.

The weather remained warm despite the heavy rain.

People with umbrellas gathered around to sing 'When the Roll is Called Up Yonder', 'The Old Rugged Cross', and other suitable songs.

Afterwards, we consumed Mannish Water (soup) with hard dough bread, and curry goat and rice. People spoke fondly of my parents, reassuring themselves that they were now 'together in the arms of the Lord'.

At home, a month after returning from the funeral, I locked myself away in our bedroom, refusing to speak to anyone phoning or visiting.

Michael acknowledged that I needed my space, although he was also hurting, and intervened only to bring me a tray, the contents of which I refused.

On the occasions I spoke, it was to snap at him, saying, 'What did you ever see in me?' or 'Why don't you leave me alone?' my eyes filling with tears of rage. On each of these occasions, I rejected Michael's attempts to comfort me.

He often found himself alone with nothing for company but the ticking of the clock on the mantle-piece.

The darkness was both indoors and out, and the winter seemed to linger.

Michael eventually released his overwhelming feelings of pain, guilt and helplessness. It was all too much for him, for me, for both of us: the passing of my parents, the miscarriage, Muhammad's and Michael's ten-day imprisonment for demonstrating, working so many hours, and the move had all been very stressful situations.

A few days later, when Michael returned from work, I was up, having showered, dressed and prepared the evening meal. We spoke for the first time since our losses, crying and comforting each other. This revitalised us both.

9

TIME OUT

*'It is through our Creator that we find out who
we are and our purpose in life.'*

Ephesians 1:1

The spring air was warm when Michael and I took ourselves away to spend two weeks in Anguilla at Mr and Mrs Edwards' secluded holiday home. This followed my parents' solemn funeral in Jamaica, which was so unlike my great uncle Louie's.

It was imperative that I travel through my emotional journey alone, with Michael there as my only companion.

It was the space and time we needed to observe and embrace the natural beauty surrounding us and to reflect, affirm and reconnect with the One who had made it all. We also needed to heal ourselves physically, psychologically, spiritually, individually and with each other as a couple, aided by prayers and meditation.

We reflected on our lives before and after we met. The greatest thing we learned was to accept that whatever we experienced, good or bad, it was important to embrace all of the emotions accompanying it. We had to learn from them, let go and move on because 'everything happened for a reason, and nothing happened before its time.'

This new way of being enabled us to be open and accept whatever life offered. For me, the respite—including fresh air, nutritious food and plenty of water— a beneficial and preferable alternative to the sometimes-unnecessary prescription of anti-depressants, which I had been on for a short while and was left in a zombie like state.

On our final night I clearly heard a faceless voice, saying, 'Up you mighty race, you can accomplish what you will.' I assumed it to be my father 'visiting' me in my dream. My father had always told my siblings and me that we could achieve whatever we put our minds to, but this wasn't his voice.

'What you do today that is worthwhile inspires others to act at some future time,' the voice continued. These were quotes I had heard before by Marcus Garvey, and wondered if it was his voice. What they meant didn't become clear to me until many years later.

Part Three

HOPE IN THE MIDST OF DESPAIR

'Always continue to climb. It is possible for you to do whatever you choose, if you first get to know who you are and are willing to work with a power that is greater than ourselves to do it.'

Oprah Winfrey

Although still mourning, Michael and I were refreshed after our trip to Anguilla. I was well enough to return to work after six weeks; however, we planned to try for another child, especially as we'd already moved from the flat into a larger house.

A year after settling into our new home, on 14 April 1991, twins Danso and Makeedah were born. Danso, who weighed seven pounds seven, was born eight minutes before Makeedah, who weighed seven pounds six.

The whole family was overjoyed. The twins truly were a blessing.

'It's sad Mum and Dad aren't here to meet their new grandchildren,' I lamented during the baby shower, which included our respective siblings, friends and a lot of food, gifts, and cards.

'They would have been very proud,' Wilfred replied.

Michael was a 'hands-on' father. In fact, if I was not around to set boundaries, the twins would have been spoilt.

Danso grew to be like me, and Makeedah, her father.

I returned to nursing on a part-time basis when the twins were in primary school, I did so until it was time for me to retire.

We continued organising and supporting events and lobbying for change on issues such as the high level of school and college exclusions, workplace harassment, unemployment and early redundancies.

Michael, Muhammad, me, and some of our friends and colleagues were particularly concerned about the number of the young people's drug and alcohol addictions, knife and gun crimes and other violence, some of which ended fatally. We were also concerned about the preoccupation with expensive technology, inappropriate fashion and violent films and music, which appeared to initiate negative attitudes and behaviours, the indulgence of which seemed to form a kind of mutual 'identity'.

Believing this problem was related to young people having no or very little parenting and/or knowledge of their ancestral history, original homeland or a sense of belonging, we designed a programme as a possible solution. It was financed through the Pardner scheme after battling with the authorities, who denied the funding despite pre-election promises to support all young people in need.

I recalled the sentiment expressed by John some years before, during our time as student nurses. He had explained how the health, education, legal and other systems were theirs: - white people. This sentiment, usually uttered behind closed doors, was being implemented, and it motivated us, along with others, to take on the responsibility of doing something about it. This was how we came up with the programme, which we called the Sankofa*[1] Programme.

The Sankofa Programme included the teaching of ancient African history and nationhood as, like in other nations, it is important for children to know their origins to foster their sense of identity, confidence, pride, purpose and legacy.

In addition to the curriculum taught in existing supplementary schools, personal development, languages and finance—including the Pardner scheme, investment and business skills—were also taught.

The participants also learnt about people of African heritage who had made positive contributions to the world, which was not taught in 'mainstream' education. Not only did this include Marcus Garvey and Amy Jacques Garvey, but also Mansa Musa, Kwame Nkrumah, Jomo Kenyatta, Patrice Lumumba, Muhumuza - queen Nyabinghi, Frederick Douglass and many others, with the plan to honour the legacy of all Africans and descendants around the world.

Older men and women taught gardening and traditional cooking, while others shared their life experiences as well as traditional African and Caribbean songs and stories. It also promoted self-help and charity.

The Programme included an annual educational retreat, in which a group of twelve young people were taken on a one-week trip to Ghana.

It was an opportunity for them to understand its history and democratic development while learning about their ancestral history and experiencing African rural, and city life.

---

[1] *Sankofa in the Ghanaian Akan language means to return and reclaim.

10

THE JOURNEY

'...the children are the future, teach them well and let them lead the way, show them all the beauty they possess inside, give them a sense of pride, to make it easier.'

George Benson

It was fortunate that our programme—the Sankofa Programme—was held on Saturday afternoons in a large room on the first floor of a community centre. It was self-financed, enabling freedom and flexibility about what it entailed and how it was organised.

The participants were young people who had either heard about it themselves and/or via their parents while attending the bookshop or through word of mouth.

The staff were dedicated volunteers, two of whom were teachers supporting a class of twelve. The afternoon would start at one o'clock with an acknowledgment of the Creator via praise and worship for ten minutes, then an hour of learning about finance/Pardner, for example. After a fifteen-minute break of fruit and drink, there would be an hour of learning about someone of African heritage who had made positive contributions, such as Harriet Tubman. The learning would include play rehearsals in preparation for a performance, with parents and others as an audience towards the end of the year. The afternoon would end with a traditional story and song.

There were some initial problems in planning the first retreat. Some of the young people were eager to experience travelling abroad for the first time. Others experienced ambivalence as their parents were resistant to their going to Africa. For some parents, it was too far away for their offspring to travel without them. A couple of parents made negative assumptions about disease, drought, violence, and kidnapping; assumptions that might not have been considered if the retreat were elsewhere in the world.

Following a four-hour plane trip from London Heathrow airport to Accra Ghana, the young participants excitedly boarded the waiting minibus on a journey to a Learning Complex – a hostel in Tema, just outside Accra, which catered for schools and colleges within and outside of Ghana. There were three bunk beds and built-in lockers in each of the eight large light and airy rooms.

We hired four rooms. The six boys shared one room and the six girls shared the other, with two twin rooms for the staff. There were communal shower cubicles, a canteen, which only provided breakfast and evening meals. There was also a 'common' room for training and meetings.

Following an itinerary of the week, the participants were up by seven o' clock and after breakfast boarded the minibus at eight thirty. Each day was spent visiting various places of interest, such as a traditional village, museums and galleries and returning for the evening meal followed by meeting in the 'common' room for reflection and discussion about the day. The free time before bedtime was spent, playing cricket, netball and table tennis or just hanging around chatting.

Those who had participated in the retreat were impressed with the country of Ghana. They particularly, admired its beautiful landscapes and the diversity of the African peoples. These included young businesspeople in their twenties and thirties who ran corporations, some large, some small, some inherited from the previous generations. Others traded within the continent and internationally.

The young participants met politicians, scientists, inventors, educators, journalists, agriculturists, artists, farmers, fishermen and craftsmen. They also visited a large family-owned business which produced poultry for sale in the supermarkets and outdoor markets around Ghana.

At a fishing port the youngsters were surprised to see strong shirtless men casting their nets into the sea and catching fish. These fishermen were unlike those they had seen on TV back in London – those who were covered head to foot in yellow waterproof wear.

They also enjoyed eating the freshly caught fish at the nearby fish restaurant. Some admitting that all the time they had eaten fish they never knew it once lived in the sea.

The group also visited a traditional village, where the people lived in wooden homes and cooked in the open air. They were self-sufficient as they drank rainwater from a water well, which was also used for irrigation. They also reared chickens and goats and grew a range of fruit and vegetables. As the community welcomed us, they killed and cooked a goat, which some of the participants were reluctant to eat as we'd seen it grazing some hours before. They did all however join in with the music and dancing which followed.

We also visited Kwame Nkrumah Memorial Park, named after the first Ghanaian president, noting the plans for Ghana's continued development. We visited the Manhyia Palace, where the participants learnt about the empires of Ashanti and Queen Yaa Asantewaa, who had mobilised her people to fight against British colonial rule.

The participants enjoyed Kakum National Park, a rainforest featuring a walk along a rope bridge.

Despite some initial resistance to crossing the bridge, completing the task turned into a successful test of strength and resilience, giving everyone a sense of achievement and instant confidence, alongside many screams, jokes, cries and laughter.

The girls within the group were particularly impressed and encouraged following a visit to a large complex which included a nursery, junior, and senior schools. These were visualised, designed and project-managed by the person who had become its headmistress then overall Principal.

The young participants also enjoyed their visit to Accra, the capital, where they felt most at home as it could have been any London high street given its diversity of peoples and shops.

The visit to the historical Elmina and Cape Coast castles in the southern region of Ghana, where some of their enslaved ancestors had been imprisoned, was the most challenging part of the educational journey of a lifetime. It was challenging for the both the younger and older visitors as they attempted to visualise what it must have been like for their distant relatives to have been shackled and crammed in the dark to the point where they were lying on top of each other, buried in each other's bodily waste and stench, not to mention the stench of those who had died within the confines of the stone-walled dungeons. Only a small window in one corner of the high wall allowed in some light. The same window was used by the overseers to throw down leftover food and view and choose which males and females to rape, as well as to watch the physical and psychological fights for survival as a form of entertainment.

The indentations on the walls and stone ground left by the shackles were evidence of the desperate attempts of the captured to escape the degradation, deprivation and humiliation - The African Holocaust!

'The Door of No Return' is a door through which was the point of exit from the castles to the sea, where the enslaved people were forcibly led to ships that took them, still shackled and crammed, to parts of the Caribbean, the Americas, Britain and elsewhere.

Part four

THE LEGACY

> *'If our people are to fight their way up out of bondage, we must arm them with pride and belief in themselves and their possibilities, based upon a sure knowledge of the achievements of the past.'*
>
> Mary McLeod Bethune

Some of those who had visualised themselves in the situations of their enslaved relatives had vowed, through eclectic emotions, to return and to reclaim their identity, and all associated with the continent. They owed it to their ancestors and would do so in their names.

Following their visit to Ghana, the young participants reflected on what they had observed and learnt. The experience was a kind of rite of passage, instilling them with a sense of history, self-awareness and pride.

All were moved by the historical knowledge of their ancestors before and after the holocaust.

They now understood their own connections to Africa. It also made sense to them that, given their physical appearances, they were its descendants. With their new knowledge, they were proud wherever they had been born and wherever they lived.

The young participants understood that aiming high and reaching their full potential was possible. They had met those who were like them in appearance who had done so, and with their new perspectives, attitudes, aspirations, self-determination and a sense of purpose, they accepted that they could too.

The Sankofa Programme, including its life-changing retreat, reorganised the young people's consciousnesses, personalities and perceptions. It also encouraged them to reconstruct new social, political and economic perspectives.

They were no longer distracted by life-destroying addictions, violence and materialism. They no longer needed to create false and negative identities for themselves and no longer depended on others to define who they ought to be.

Those who had participated in the Sankofa Programme—and those who did not but had a strong connection to their families—were aware of the importance of heritage on which identity and self-respect are based. They also learnt the importance of faith, purpose, unity, creativity, self-determination, cooperation, working together, responsibility and the desire to focus on the support, development and maintenance of the family, community and nation (just as it is acceptable for the other nations).

'Education is the most powerful weapon which you can use to change the world.'

Nelson Mandela

I was fifty-five when I retired from nursing. I was a Sister and had no ambitions to further my career. I enjoyed being hands-on with patients as well as staff in the thirty-odd years I was at St Luke's. Retiring meant I had more time to spend in the Sankofa Programme.

Michael, on the other hand, continued in education on a part-time basis until he retired at sixty-five. He also remained committed to the Sankofa Programme, preparing for the next generation to inherit it.

We planned to emigrate to Ghana because life there seemed more relaxed. Michael had relatives there, and we had made friends during our honeymoon and during the Sankofa retreats.

Two of the visits included overseeing work being done on the house we had purchased in 1995 from a Mr Johnson, an African-American who had lived in Ghana with his wife for many years until she passed away. His decision to sell the house was because he was returning to live in America with his daughter and her family.

We emigrated to Ghana in the spring of 2011. Our children—Danso and Makeedah, who were 20—had been raised with our principles and values and attended every retreat since childhood, took over the running of the Sankofa Programme. They did so with those who had previously participated – some who had later studied agriculture, biodiversity, architecture, economics, engineering, forestry, medicine, science, law, technology, media and other subjects. There were also those who owned and ran successful corporations and invented and manufactured products and services from 'womb to tomb', creating opportunities for employment and apprenticeships. They had seized the opportunity to improve the quality of their lives and the lives of others.

The Sankofa Programme was no longer exclusive to 'troubled' young people. It had expanded, with branches in the Caribbean, the Americas, Europe, Kenya, Mali, The Gambia, Australia, New Zealand and the Pacific Islands.

The money generated contributed to financing and developing land, building homes and education, health and other institutions and industries around the world. Thankfully, Michael, Muhammad, Victor, myself, and others had focused on what and who mattered despite the obstacles, without fear or favour. We had implemented the African proverb urging us to 'Act as if it is impossible to fail!'

EPILOGUE

'Success always leaves footprints.'

Booker T. Washington

'Grandad!' called Danso's sons, Kwame and Kehinde. They ran towards Michael as he approached the veranda, wearing mud and grass-stained overalls. His build was full, his hair and moustache intertwined with grey. 'Hello, twins,' he said, still unable to tell which was which.

After laying down the sack of fresh fish, fruit and vegetables Michael had gathered from the nearby family plot, he lightly kissed the foreheads of Makeedah's daughters, Abena and Afryea, as well as mine.

As a couple, we were still strong in mind, body and spirit and still in love, now resembling each other as longtime spouses often do.

The laughing children updated Michael about the presence of the photo album, retrieving earlier photos of him and me sporting 1970s and 80s fashion.

'You were so beautiful. Like a king and queen,' Abena said, admiring our wedding photos. The other children agreed.

'I've always told your grandmother that she was my queen,' Michael told them, gently taking my hand and kissing me on the cheek. He sang the chorus of 'Queen Majesty' (by The Techniques).

Smiling coyly, I tapped Michael's arm gently, pretending not to appreciate his affection for me.

'You really, really do love Granddad, don't you, Granny?' Afryea asked, giggling with the other children.

'Of course I do, even after all these years.' I blushed upon recalling the first time Michael had sung that song to me.

After taking Michael a cool drink, I withdrew to the kitchen to prepare the late afternoon meal, utilising the fresh produce.

Michael told the grandchildren stories he made up about their parents when they were children. He continued, with them laughing until they ached. Both sets of parents—Danso and his wife, Imarni, and Makeedah and her husband, Delroy Junior—arrived, as did my siblings, Dr Winston Walker, who was retired, his wife, Shola, and twelve-year-old grandson. Faith, a retired nurse, her husband, Bentley, and three grandchildren also arrived, as did Wilfred, a retired engineer, his wife, Paulette, and their two children, and Michael's sister, Melanie, having all returned from sightseeing and shopping in Accra.

Mr and Mrs Edwards, who lived in Anguilla not far from Muhammad, his wife, Nia, and their two sons and two granddaughters, also visited.

Michael sat at the head of the table, and I sat opposite him as he blessed the meal: 'For health and strength and daily food, we praise thy name, oh Lord. Amen.'

The large table, placed on the lawn under the umbrella of a mango tree, was covered in white linen, which I'd embroidered.

Displayed on it was a plate of fried chicken and fish and bowls of stewed chicken, ackee and salt fish, fufu, jollof rice and rice and peas. There was also yam, green bananas, fried plantain, avocado and salad, all of which were washed down with home-grown fruit transformed into delicious, non-alcoholic cocktails.

It became comfortably warm in the evening, and the voices of the insects were more audible.

The male adults and children played football whilst the female adults cleared, washed up, and tidied everything away, chatting, singing and laughing. The gendered division of labour was unplanned, unquestioned and okay.

The stars glistened like diamonds in the navy velvet sky above the silhouette of the trees as the contented family and close friends relaxed on the illuminated veranda below.

Michael and I were presented with gifts in celebration of our Ruby wedding anniversary, which included a series of children's books in the latest format as well as glossy hardbacks.

Printed on the covers and inside pages were 'Written by Michael Mensah' and 'Illustrated by Patience Walker-Mensah.' We had no idea the stories we'd made up about our children all those years ago would be read by so many people around the world.

'Happy forty years!' our family and friends cheered, lifting their glasses in celebration.

The late evening concluded with singing and dancing to eclectic music, including soukous and reggae.

The following afternoon, once the visitors had returned to their respective residences in England, Anguilla and America, the detached home in Kumasi, where we had lived for the past sixteen years, had become silent.

That night, as I lay by Michael's side, I thought about the list I had drawn up in Jamaica all those years ago, ticking each item off in my mind: I had met and married the kind, caring, considerate, and supportive man I'd requested; and we had two beautiful children, grandchildren, and a comfortable home. We had accomplished our purpose, which included the Sankofa Programme.

I gave thanks to the One who had made it all possible.

Two years later, at the age of eighty-five, following a heart attack, Michael visited me in a dream. He stood in front of me smiling, his arms stretched out towards me. I allowed them to enfold me, and I felt warm and safe.

Michael whispered, 'I still love you, my queen.' He kissed my cheek.

'Thank you for being my husband and for the wonderful life we had together,' I whispered in return.

When I awoke, I turned—the space in the bed next to me was empty. I remembered the warmth, peace and contentment I'd felt and was reassured that Michael was okay and watching over me and all those he loved.

Feeling immensely tired and weary I fell asleep again. Suddenly, I heard the voice I had heard before in a dream. It said, 'Thank you. You and those around you have contributed to making a difference. You have accomplished all you could have towards a better world. The next generation will continue. Now rest and be at peace.'

THE END

ABOUT THE AUTHOR

𝓑arbara has two sons and lives in London. During the 2020 lockdown, she reflected on her life, which resulted in her deciding to take early retirement from a career as a social worker and psychotherapist and pursue her dream of becoming a writer.

In her spare time, she is a member of her local community choir and volunteers at a homeless project. The story of Patience gives an insight into what life was like for children of Windrush parents.

Conscious Dreams
PUBLISHING

Transforming diverse writers
into successful published authors

www.consciousdreamspublishing.com

authors@consciousdreamspublishing.com

Let's connect

www.ingramcontent.com/pod-product-compliance
Lightning Source LLC
Chambersburg PA
CBHW050203130526
44591CB00034B/2081